Machines at work

LB1

Monster machines

AXIS education

Acknowledgments

Photographs: page 3 © Komatsu; pages 5 and 11 © Giant Excavator; page 7 © Tim Minelli; page 9 © DGK80; page 13 © Nemjez; page 15 © Thyssen Krupp; page 17 © K-Tec Earthmovers; pages 19 and 33 © Volvo; page 21 © K W Slovachek; page 23 © Wei Chun; page 25 © Lawrence Soto & Frank Wells; page 27 © Joe Gavlas; page 29 © Cov Ltwt; page 31 © David Friel and © lildodgey; page 35 © Intel Free Press; page 37 © John Deere.

Every effort has been made to contact copyright holders of material reproduced in this book. Any omissions will be rectified in subsequent printings if notice is given to the publishers.

Copyright © Axis Education 2012

All rights reserved; no part of this publication may be reproduced, stored in a retrieval system, transmitted in any form, or by any means, electronic, mechanical, photocopying, recording or otherwise, without the prior permission of the publisher.

First published in Great Britain by Axis Education Ltd.

ISBN 978-1-84618-302-7

Axis Education
PO Box 459
Shrewsbury
SY4 4WZ

Email: enquiries@axiseducation.co.uk

www.axiseducation.co.uk

Monster machines

This book is full of information about the longest, heaviest and biggest machines in their class. Monster machines are used to either move a lot of people or things in a shorter amount of time than it would take using a smaller version of the same machine. For example, in Beijing traffic is very busy because lots of people need to move about. So a Chinese company has made an extra long bus that can take 300 passengers at a time compared to a standard bus that carries 50.

Monster bulldozers are used for huge construction jobs when a lot of earth needs to be moved with a huge blade. So, whether it's a passenger bus, a fire engine or massive earth moving gear, you'll find all sorts of information about monster machines in this book.

This Komatsu bulldozer has a 6.21m long blade.

Machines at work

One of the biggest dumper trucks ever built is the Caterpillar 797F. It's used to carry huge loads of mining waste – usually rubble from coal, copper, iron or gold mining. When the truck is loaded its top speed is 42 miles per hour.

The Caterpillar 797F is too heavy to drive on a regular road. It is so big that it takes 12 to 13 lorries to deliver the machine in pieces to the site where it will be used. A team of mechanics go to the site to put the machine together. It takes the mechanics 7–10 days to weld the dumper body together. After that, another seven mechanics work around-the-clock shifts to assemble the truck, taking 20 more days to complete the job.

If a 797F has to be moved from one job site to another, it must be taken apart and put back together again. With its payload capacity of 363 tonnes the Caterpillar 797F is classified as an 'ultra class' machine. The ultra class covers all haul trucks with a payload capacity of 272 tonnes or more.

Monster machines

The Caterpillar 797F.

Owning a 797F isn't cheap. The price of each machine varies, but will set you back £2.5-4 million. Each tyre costs about £26,500. The machine also takes 3,785 litres of fuel – that means it will cost over £5,000 to fill the tank!

Machines at work

Massive dumper trucks need equally large machines to load them. The Le Torneau L-2350 is the biggest wheel loader in the world. The shovel bucket is 7.3 metres wide and has a very large capacity of 48 cubic metres. That means it can move about 72 tonnes of material with just one scoop.

With a 7.3 metre lift height and a 3.5 metre reach, the L-2350 is able to lift massive quantities of rocks and rubble, or waste into giant dumper trucks. The L-2350 is designed to work in an open cast mine where it will shovel thousands of tonnes of material every day. Just like the Caterpillar 797F dumper truck, the L-2350 is so big that it has to be put together on site.

The whole point of having a machine this large is to cope with rocks in huge quantities and to speed up mining. The L-2350 can load a 362 tonne truck in just five passes, a 290 tonne truck in only four passes and 72 tonne truck, of course, is filled in just one pass. Costing £4.7 million to buy and using up to 4,773 litres of fuel in 24 hours going at just 5 miles per hour, it's far from cheap though.

Le Tourneau L-2350 fitted with snow chains.

Firestone developed the 70/70-57 SRG DT tyre especially for the L-2350. Le Tourneau and Firestone claim it is the largest tyre ever made. It has an overall diameter of 4 metres and is 1.78 metres wide. The tyres cost £39,000 each. If you're lucky enough to see this machine in action, you may see it fitted with snow chains. Chains not only help with traction on muddy or snowy ground, but they also protect the tyres from damage.

Machines at work

Bulldozers clear the ground ready for building. For moving massive amounts of earth or rubble you may need to use a huge machine. One of the biggest production bulldozers is the Komatsu D575A. A production machine is one that is made as part of a batch in a factory. Komatsu stopped making the machine in 2012. The last one was delivered to work in a mine in Australia.

The Komatsu D575A is 4.8 metres high, 12.5 metres long and 7.3 metres wide. Its blade alone is 7.4 metres wide and 3.3 metres tall – that's not much smaller than a London bus.

This machine doesn't move quickly. With just three gears its top speed going forwards is 7.5 miles per hour. It goes faster in reverse with a top speed of 8.6 miles per hour. It may be slow, but with the blade down, this bulldozer will crush anything in its way. Those who use it say the D575A is built to knock down mountains!

Monster machines

It takes more than one extra strong engine to tow this massive beast!

Transporting the D575A isn't easy. It can be taken apart to move it, but with the help of two huge lorry cabs and a giant low loader it can also be towed in one piece via road.

Machines at work

Monster machines tend to work in some of the world's toughest places. The biggest hydraulic digger is the RH400. It's used for extreme digging in places such as the Artic or in huge mines.

You need to be skilled to work this machine. Even though it's big, the bucket is controlled by a touch of the finger. It can be moved with extreme accuracy because the controls are so sensitive. There is plenty of comfort for the driver too. There is an air-conditioned, spacious cab with good visibility and a comfy seat. There is even a small kitchen for the driver to use when he or she is taking a break!

The RH400 is massive. It's 10 metres high, 9 metres wide and 19 metres long – making it bigger than the average house in the UK. The machine weighs in at 977 tonnes and has a shovel capacity of 85 tonnes. It's fast too – it can pick up about 8,200 tonnes of material an hour. A single scoop of the 52m^3 volume shovel shifts 90 tonnes of rock. The shovel size is an exact match to the payload capacity of a heavy duty vehicle, so it can fill the truck with just one scoop.

Monster machines

The RH400 costs a cool £7,000,000.

The RH400 is in daily use at the Twin Creeks gold mine in Nevada in the United States. It's a surface gold mine, so tonnes of soil have to be moved to find the gold.

Machines at work

Bucket wheel excavators are used to dig at the earth's surface. They are huge, heavy machines that dig around the clock in open pits. Strong wires lower the wheel to the ground. As the wheel turns, sharp-toothed buckets scoop up the material being mined. In a coal mine, most bucket wheel excavators can scoop about 40,000 buckets of coal in just one day. The buckets tip out their load onto a moving belt when they get to the top of the wheel. Material is carried along the belt and is transported away by truck or train. The excavator moves very slowly on massive crawler tracks.

Depending on what they are being used for, the boom length on a bucket wheel excavator can be from as short as 6 metres to as long as 80 metres.

Monster machines

The buckets on a bucket wheel excavator have a sharp cutting edge to dig up material.

The biggest bucket wheel excavator is Bagger 293. It's used at a brown coal mine in Hambach, Germany. The mine employs over one thousand people and is on an area of 100 square miles. Bagger 293 took five years to design and make and another five years to build on site.

Bagger 293 stands 96 metres tall – that's more than twice as tall as Nelson's Column. This monster is 225 metres long and weighs 12,882 tonnes. The bucket wheel alone is over 21 metres high and has 20 buckets which can each hold 15 cubic metres of coal. Bagger 293 can move over 2.6 million cubic metres of earth per day. Amazingly, it only needs five people to work the machine, one of which drives a dumper truck.

Monster machines

Bagger 293.

You can get some idea of the size of this giant by looking at how small the people are in the picture – they are tiny.

Machines at work

Road building involves the use of a range of large machines. A scraper is used to remove the top, uneven layer from the ground. Scrapers are also used for other construction jobs where earth needs to be moved over short distances (up to about two miles) over relatively smooth areas.

The biggest scraper in the world is currently the K-Tec 1254 ADT. It can scrape massive amounts of earth with a heaped capacity of 54 cubic metres. The 1254 ADT is designed to be pulled by a 36-tonne, 450+ horsepower truck.

The K-Tec 1254 uses special high tensile steel plating. This strengthened metal means that the machine has an extremely durable scraper – it is far stronger than most competing machines. The cutting edge is 4.27 metres wide.

Monster machines

You can judge the scale of the 1254 from this picture!

The K-Tec 1254 at work.

17

Machines at work

Once the scraper has done its job, the second stage of road building is for a compactor to use its heavy wheels to make the earth flat. After that a grader uses a big metal blade to smooth a flat layer of small stones. Once all the preparation work is done the road is surfaced using a paver and a roller.

The paver spreads a layer of asphalt, or tarmac, over the road. It has a container at the front called a hopper which is filled with the asphalt. As the paver moves along, the asphalt falls from the back. Dumper trucks fill the paver with more asphalt as it is needed.

The asphalt is warm as it is poured from the paver onto the ground. The roller drives behind the paver and flattens the tarmac which sets hard as it cools.

Monster machines

The Volvo ABG9820 paver working on a new motorway.

This heavy duty Volvo paver is used to lay tarmac in all sorts of places!

Concrete is a mixture of chalk, stones, sand and water. Mini-concrete mixers are used for small building jobs. Large construction sites usually have concrete delivered in a mixer. The concrete is mixed in a big revolving drum on the back of the lorry. There are paddles inside the drum that constantly turn the concrete mixture.

A big advantage of the cement mixer truck is that a large amount of concrete can be delivered in a short space of time. When the lorry arrives at the site the mixture is ready for pouring. The driver presses a switch so that the drum moves in the opposite direction. The paddles inside the drum then scoop the mixture towards the mouth of the drum and onto the exit chute.

The driver won't want to get stuck in traffic because there is a limit to the amount of time the concrete can remain in the mixing drum. No matter how much it is churned, in time concrete will become thick and turn hard. In an emergency the driver can add chemicals to slow the hardening down until he or she arrives at the site. The size of the mixer will depend on the amount of concrete needed. The biggest mixers can carry as much as 20 cubic metres of concrete.

Monster machines

As soon as the concrete arrives on site it must be placed, levelled, compacted and finished – usually within an hour or two. So as well as working out how much concrete to have delivered, the site manager also needs to have enough workers to do the job in time before the concrete becomes unworkable.

An extra large American concrete mixer.

Tower cranes are already very tall machines, but by far the biggest tower crane in the world is the Kroll K-10000. At 120 metres high this Danish made crane towers above all others. It is more than three times bigger and stronger than any tower crane ever built.

The K-10000 isn't the newest of cranes. It was first made in the 1980s to help build nuclear power stations. Nowadays these giants are used in shipyards, regular power stations and for taking oil platforms apart. People still want the K-10000 because it is so efficient – it can cut six to nine months off a four-year construction phase of a power plant, which adds up to a good deal of money.

The crane is made of steel. Its base is 12 metres in diameter. The crane has three sections and all joints are welded to the highest standard. Once the welding is done, the surface goes through a three-stage process. Firstly it is shot-blasted with steel sand to clean it, then it is sprayed with a mix of molten aluminium and zinc. Finally it gets a coat of special protective paint in the customer's choice of colour. This careful process means that the crane will last a long time without any rust problems and will need little maintenance. As with any huge structure, this crane takes time to put together – almost a year.

Monster machines

The K-10000 at work in a shipyard in Singapore, note the small crane within the crane!

Machines at work

When finished and fixed to the ground the K-10000 weighs a total of 202 tonnes. The crane is incredibly strong and can withstand winds of 149mph. It has a maximum jib reach of 100 metres, it lifts 85 tonnes at the tip end. The winch has a 10,000kg line pull. The maximum line speed is 50 metres per minute with a 12 tonne load.

You can still buy the K-10000 new – it costs about £6 million. If you can get your hands on a used one, expect to pay £1 million to £2 million, depending on the condition it's in.

Kroll has plans for an even bigger crane. No one has ordered the K-25000 yet, but this is a 363 tonne crane capable of lifting 181 tonnes out to a radius of 100 metres with a maximum single point lift of 363 tonnes at a 57 metre reach.

If you are interested in the K-25000, plan to spend more than £8 million.

Monster machines

You would expect tower cranes to be large, but it may come as a surprise that mobile cranes can be huge too. In America the LTL-2600 Transi-Lift crane was used to build one of the world's largest factories for Intel, the computer company. It was the biggest mobile crane in the world at the time. It took 220 low-loaders to move the crane in pieces to the factory site in Oregon. Workers took four weeks to put the crane together. With the attached jibs it can stretch up to 213 metres and lifts 2,140 tonnes in one lift – that's more than 600 large male elephants!

The LTL-2600 Transi-Lift with just the main jib visible.

There were fifteen cranes working on the Intel site which used about 40,823 tonnes of steel. The finished building is eight times larger than America's biggest supermarket building, Walmart. But the LTL-2600 crane towered above all the other cranes on site. In fact it was about twice as tall as all of them and took several cranes to put it together in the first place. What makes this crane unique is that it can move on crawler tracks while it is lifting.

The LTL-2600 won't be the biggest mobile crane for long though. Lampson has plans to make a Transi-Lift LTL-3000 which will be used to help build a nuclear power plant for the Tokyo Electric Power Company. It will be 20% more capable than the LTL-2600 with new winches and larger wire that will increase it's lifting power by 20% and its hoisting speed by 50%.

Monster machines

The LTL-2600 Transi-lift on site at the Intel factory in Oregon.

Machines at work

In Britain a 25 metre double-trailer lorry claims to be the longest lorry in the UK. The machine is owned by Denby Transport, a Lincoln based transport company.

The lorry cost £100,000 and is 8 metres longer than a standard lorry. It has eight axles instead of the usual six. When empty it weighs 22 tonnes, instead of 16. This lorry has 50% more capacity than a standard articulated lorry.

Denby had planned to use the lorry to carry lightweight goods such as aluminium cans, cereal and crisps. That way the lorry load would stay within the maximum weight of 44 tonnes for UK roads.

However, on its first outing in 2009 the driver was stopped by police and then questioned by the Vehicle and Operator Services Agency (VOSA). They believed that the lorry exceeded British road safety rules, even though it was within the weight limit.

Monster machines

We're unlikely to see double trailers on our roads any time soon.

Lorries as long as the Denby-owned model currently travel on roads in Sweden, Finland and Holland. The double-trailer lorry saves on fuel and cuts CO^2 emissions by 16–18%. Denby Transport saw it as a way to reduce the number of lorries on British motorways and to be more efficient. However, due to road safety issues, it seems unlikely that VOSA will allow these long loads to travel on British roads anytime soon.

Machines at work

One of the biggest vehicles you are likely to see regularly in the UK is a fire engine. They are large because they need room for a fire crew as well as equipment for putting out fires. The equipment weighs about one and a half tonnes. Inside there is a tank for as much as 2,000 litres of water too. Fire engines usually carry flood lights and are fitted with pumps. Some have cutting machines and glass kits for dealing with traffic accidents.

Some engines have an extendable platform that can reach up to the windows of tall buildings. Others have sets of extendable ladders. A popular platform is the Bronto Skylift because it has a big rescue platform but is very compact. The Bronto Skylift is controlled electronically so it's easy and safe to use.

Monster machines

An Angloco Fire Engine used by Shropshire Fire and Rescue Service.

Fire crews in Rhyl doing drills with the Bronto lift extended.

Machines at work

You may have thought that the bendy bus in London was likely to be the longest bus ever. However, transport problems in China's biggest cities have prompted the Youngman Vehicle Group to create the JNP6250G. This massive bus is 25 metres long and has three sections. It has five doors and just forty seats, but it can carry 300 passengers.

The JNP6250G travels on the roads of Beijing and Hangzhou in bus only lanes. At 25 metres long it is 13 metres longer than most buses and its top speed is 50mph. It has concertina style hinges so it can turn corners with the same radius as a normal bus. In London the hinges of the bendy bus were a danger to pedestrians and cyclists, but in China special bus lanes have been built for Youngman's extra long bus.

China isn't the only country using articulated buses. Volvo has sold its buses in Australia, Europe and South America. Their 7300 bus is also 25 metres long but it can carry just 240 passengers.

Monster machines

The Volvo 7300 waiting for passengers at a Mexican bus stop.

In Mexico, 135 of these extra long buses will be used on special bus-ways. Mexico City has the world's longest corridor of bus-ways with almost 18 miles that connect the north part of the city to the south. The city plans to create eleven new bus-ways over the next five years that will cover almost 150 miles.

Machines at work

Farmers often need to do a lot of work in a short space of time. Tractors are used to pull machines to dig up ground, plant seeds and spray crops. The biggest tractor ever made was called Big Bud 747. It was built in 1977 to plough huge cotton fields. Moving at 8 miles per hour Big Bud 747 can plough one acre every minute. That is very fast for a tractor.

Big Bud is 8.7 metres long, 4.3 metres high, 6.4 metres wide and has a wheelbase of 5 metres. It weighs 40 tonnes with a full tank of diesel. Big Bud has a 24.1 litre Detroit V16 92 Turbo engine delivering 900hp. It has six forward and one reverse gear driving 2.4 metre tall wheels.

This tractor isn't a working model any more, but people from all over the world still come to see it at a museum in Iowa.

Monster machines

People from all over the world go to see Big Bud 747.

Machines at work

When crops are ready they must be harvested right away. Before machines, huge teams of workers were needed to do this. These days huge combine harvesters can do the work of lots of people.

John Deere is the world's biggest manufacturer of combines and it also makes the S690 – one of the world's biggest combines. This machine is built for European crops. It has the most powerful engine in a combine today, with a massive 625 horsepower. It also has a 10 tonne capacity, making this the largest grain tank too. With such a large tank the driver can work longer before stopping to empty the load. What's more, when the tank is full the grain can be emptied in just 105 seconds. The S-Series can travel on the road at a top speed of 18mph. New for 2012, those lucky enough to drive it say that the machine is bigger, faster and better at its job than other machines. It's also easy to use and is very comfortable – it even has a fridge to keep food and drink cool.

Monster machines

The John Deere S690 is one of biggest combine harvesters in the world.

Machines at work

Glossary

ADT	abbreviation for articulated dumper truck
advantage	a good or useful quality or condition that something has
aluminium	a silver-white metal that is very light
articulated	a machine with two sections connected with a flexible joint that allows the machine to turn more sharply
assemble	to put something together
asphalt	a hard, black substance used to make roads and paths
CO_2 emissions	carbon dioxide gas that is produced when fuel is burned. CO_2 emissions are a cause of global warming
compacted	pressed together so something becomes tight or solid
concertina	something that folds together on itself
construction	building works
diameter	a straight line that goes from one side of a circle to the other side and through the centre, or the length of this line
excavator	another word for a digger
extendable	something that can be made longer
high tensile	something that can take a great deal of pressure before it will break
hoisting speed	how quickly a crane can hoist goods
horsepower/hp	a unit for measuring the power of an engine
levelled	having been made flat
maintenance	work that is done to keep something in good condition

manufacturer	a company that produces a product
molten	metal or rock that has been heated to form a liquid state
pass	the act of moving past something, so moving one scoop of earth, for example
payload	the carrying capacity of a vehicle
pedestrian	a person who is walking and not travelling in a vehicle
radius	a certain distance from a particular point in any direction
revolving	a straight line that goes from one side of a circle to the other side and through the centre, or the length of this line
servicing	examining and repairing a machine
shot-blasted	to clean with a machine that blows sand out at a high speed
traction	the ability to hold the ground without sliding
visibility	how far or how well you can see
VOSA	the Vehicle and Operator Services Agency responsible for road safety in the UK